In the Year 1920

By

Kerry Butters.

In the Year 1920.

Millennium:	2nd millennium
Centuries:	19th century – **20th century** – 21st century
Decades:	1890s 1900s 1910s – **1920s** – 1930s 1940s 1950s
Years:	1917 1918 1919 – **1920** – 1921 1922 1923

1920 (MCMXX) was a leap year starting on Thursday (dominical letter DC) of the Gregorian calendar and a leap year starting on Wednesday (dominical letter ED) of the Julian calendar, the 1920th year of the Common Era (CE) and *Anno Domini* (AD) designations, the 920th year of the 2nd millennium, the 20th year of the 20th century, and the 1st year of the 1920s decade. Note that the Julian day for 1920 is 13 calendar days difference, which continued to be used from 1582 until the complete conversion of the Gregorian calendar was entirely done in 1929.

Contents

Events

January

- January – 4,025 suspected communists and anarchists arrested and held without trial in the United States following raids in several cities.
- January 1
  - Babe Ruth is traded by the Red Sox for $125,000, the largest sum ever paid for a player at that time.
  - Bolsheviks increase troops from four divisions to twenty along the Polish border
- January 7
  - The forces of Russian White Admiral Alexander Kolchak surrender in Krasnoyarsk. The Great Siberian Ice March ensues.
  - The New York State Assembly refuses to seat five duly elected Socialist assemblymen.
- January 9 – Thousands of onlookers watch as "The Human Fly" George Polley climbs the Woolworth Building in New York City. He reaches the 30th floor before being arrested.

- January 10 – League of Nations Covenant enters into force. On January 16 the organization holds its first council meeting, in Paris.
- January 11 – The Azerbaijan Democratic Republic is recognised de facto by European powers in Versailles.
- January 13 – *The New York Times* ridicules the American rocket scientist Robert H. Goddard. The newspaper has to recant publicly on July 17, 1969 when the Apollo crew is on its mission to the Moon.
- January 16
    - Prohibition in the United States begins with the Eighteenth Amendment to the Constitution coming into effect.
    - The Allies of World War I demand that the Netherlands extradite the German Kaiser Wilhelm II, who fled there in 1918.
    - Zeta Phi Beta Sorority, Incorporated, is founded on the campus of Howard University in Washington, D.C.
- January 19 – The United States Senate votes against joining the League of Nations.
- January 22 – The Australian Country Party is officially formed, led by Nelson Pollard.
- January 23 – The Netherlands refuses to extradite the German Kaiser.
- January 28 – *El Tercio de Extranjeros*, the "Regiment of Foreigners", later the Spanish Legion, is established by decree of King Alfonso XIII of Spain.
- January 30 – The oldest surviving pro wrestling match on film takes place, with Joe Stecher defeating Earl Caddock.

February

- February 2
  - Estonian War of Independence: The Tartu Peace Treaty is signed, ending the war and recognizing Estonian independence.
  - France occupies Memel.
  - Sayyid Muhammad, Khan of Khiva abdicates.
- February 7 – Admiral Kolchak and Viktor Pepelyayev are executed by firing squad near Irkutsk.
- February 9 – The Svalbard Treaty, signed by members of the League of Nations in Paris, recognises the sovereignty of Norway over the Arctic archipelago of Svalbard (at this time called Spitzbergen) while giving the other signatories economic rights in the islands.
- February 10 – General Józef Haller first performs Poland's Wedding to the Sea, a symbolic celebration of the restitution of Polish access to the Baltic Sea.
- February 12–24 – Conference of London: Leaders of the United Kingdom, France and Italy meet to discuss the partitioning of the Ottoman Empire.
- February 13 – Switzerland rejoins the League of Nations.
- February 14 – The League of Women Voters is founded in Chicago.
- February 17 – A woman named Anna Anderson tries to commit suicide in Berlin and is taken to a mental hospital, where she claims she is Grand Duchess Anastasia of Russia.
- February 19 – The United States Senate refuses to ratify the Treaty of Versailles.

- February 20 – 1920 Gori earthquake: An earthquake hits Gori in the Democratic Republic of Georgia, killing 114.
- February 21 – The island province of Marinduque in the Philippines archipelago is founded.
- February 22 – In Emeryville, California, the first dog racing track to employ an imitation rabbit opens.
- February 24 – Adolf Hitler presents his National Socialist Program in Munich to the German Workers' Party (*Deutsche Arbeiterpartei*) which renames itself as the Nazi Party (*Nationalsozialistische Deutsche Arbeiterpartei*).

March

- March 1
    - Hungarian Admiral and statesman Miklós Horthy becomes the Regent of Hungary.
    - The United States Railroad Administration returns control of American railroads to its constituent railroad companies.
- March 7 – Syrian National Congress proclaims Syria independent with Faisal I of Iraq as king.
- March 10
    - The world's first peaceful establishment of a social democratic government takes place in Sweden. Hjalmar Branting takes over when Nils Edén leaves office.
    - The Baylor Business Men's Club changes its name to the Baylor University Chamber of Commerce.
- March 13–17 – Wolfgang Kapp and Walther von Lüttwitz's 'Kapp Putsch', an attempted coup in Germany, briefly ousts

the Weimar Republic government from Berlin but fails due to public resistance and a general strike.
- March 15 – The Ruhr Red Army, a communist army 60,000 men strong, is formed in Germany.
- March 15–16 – Military occupation of Constantinople by British Empire forces acting for the Allied Powers against the Turkish National Movement. Retrospectively, the Grand National Assembly of Turkey regards this as the dissolution of the Ottoman regime in Istanbul.
- March 17 – Birthday of Bangabandhu Sheikh Mujibur Rahman, father of the nation of Bangladesh and a political leader (d. 1975)
- March 18 – Greece begins using the Gregorian calendar.
- March 19 – The United States Congress refuses to ratify the Treaty of Versailles.
- March 23 – Admiral Miklós Horthy declares that Hungary is a monarchy without anyone on the throne.
- March 25 – Irish War of Independence: British recruits to the Royal Irish Constabulary begin to arrive in Ireland. They become known from their improvised uniforms as the "Black and Tans".
- March 26 – The German government asks France for permission to use its own troops against the rebellious Ruhr Red Army in the French-occupied area.
- March 28 – The 1920 Palm Sunday tornado outbreak hits the Great Lakes region and Deep South of the United States.
- March 29 – Sir William Robertson is promoted to Field Marshal, the first man to rise from private (enlisted 1877) to the highest rank in the British Army.

April

- April 2 – The German army marches to the Ruhr to fight the Ruhr Red Army.
- April 4 – 1920 Palestine riots: Violence erupts between Arab and Jewish residents in Jerusalem; 9 killed, 216 injured.
- April 6 – The short-lived Far Eastern Republic is declared in eastern Siberia.
- April 11 – Mexican Revolution: Álvaro Obregón flees from Mexico City during a trial intended to ruin his reputation; he flees to Guerrero where he joins Fortunato Maycotte.
- April 19–26 – San Remo conference: Representatives of Italy, France, the United Kingdom and Japan meet to determine the League of Nations mandates for administration of territories following partitioning of the Ottoman Empire.
- April 19 – Germany and Bolshevist Russia agree to the exchange of prisoners of war.

1920 Summer Olympics

- April 20
  - Mexican Revolution: Álvaro Obregón announces in Chilpancingo that he intends to fight against the rule of Venustiano Carranza.

- The 1920 Summer Olympics open in Antwerp, Belgium. The Olympic symbols of five interlocking rings and the associated flag are first displayed at the games.
- April 23 – The Grand National Assembly of Turkey is founded by Mustafa Kemal Atatürk in Ankara. It denounces the government of Sultan Mehmed VI and announces a temporary constitution.
- April 24 – Polish–Soviet War: Polish and anti-Soviet Ukrainian troops attack the Red Army in Soviet Ukraine.
- April 26 – The Khorezm People's Soviet Republic is officially created by Bolshevist Russia as the successor to the Khanate of Khiva.
- April 28 – The Azerbaijan Soviet Socialist Republic is officially created.

May

- May 2 – The first game of Negro National League baseball is played in Indianapolis, Indiana.
- May 3 – A Bolshevik coup fails in the Democratic Republic of Georgia.
- May 7
  - Polish–Soviet War: Polish troops occupy Kiev. The government of the Ukrainian People's Republic returns to the city.
  - Mexican Revolution: Venustiano Carranza leaves Mexico City in a large train.

- Treaty of Moscow (1920): Soviet Russia recognizes independence of the Democratic Republic of Georgia only to invade the country six months later.
- May 15 – Russian Revolution: Russian White soldier Maria Bochkareva is executed in Soviet Russia.
- May 16
    - Canonization of Joan of Arc. Over 30,000 people attend the ceremony in Rome, including 140 descendants of Joan of Arc's family. Pope Benedict XV presides over the rite, for which the interior of St. Peter's Basilica in Rome is richly decorated.
    - A referendum in Switzerland is favorable to joining the League of Nations.
- May 17
    - French and Belgian troops leave the cities they have occupied in Germany.
    - The first flight of Dutch air company KLM, from Amsterdam to London, takes place.
- May 19 – Mexican Revolution: Álvaro Obregón's troops enter Mexico City.
- May 20 – Mexican Revolution: Venustiano Carranza arrives in San Antonio Tlaxcalantongo. Troops of Rodolfo Herrero attack him at night and shoot him.
- May 24 – Venustiano Carranza is buried in Mexico City; all of his mourning allies are arrested. Adolfo de la Huerta is elected provisional president.
- May 26 – Ganja revolt: Anti-Soviet opposition in the Azerbaijan SSR launches an abortive revolt in Ganja.
- May 27 – Tomáš Garrigue Masaryk becomes president of Czechoslovakia.

- May 29 – Great Floods at Louth, Lincolnshire in England kill 23.

June

- June 4 – Treaty of Trianon: Peace is restored between the Allied Powers and Hungary. Hungary loses 72% of its territory.
- June 5 – Bolshevik Cavalry break through Polish and Ukrainian lines south of Kiev, precipitating eventual withdrawal.
- June 12 – Polish–Soviet War: The Red Army retakes Kiev.
- June 13
  - Essad Pasha Toptani, nominal ruler of Albania, is assassinated by Avni Rustemi in Paris.
  - The United States Post Office Department rules that children may not be sent via parcel post.
- June 15 – A new border treaty between Germany and Denmark gives northern Schleswig to Denmark.
- June 22 – Greek Summer Offensive: Greece attacks Turkish troops.

July

- July 1 – Germany declares its neutrality in the war between Poland and Soviet Russia.
- July 2 – Polish–Soviet War: Red Army continues offensive into Poland.
- July 7 – Arthur Meighen becomes Canada's ninth prime minister.

- July 11 – In the East Prussian plebiscite the local populace decides to remain with Weimar Germany.
- July 12 – Soviet–Lithuanian Peace Treaty: The Russian Soviet Federative Socialist Republic recognizes independent Lithuania.
- July 13 – London County Council bars foreigners from council jobs.
- July 19 – August 7 – The Second Congress of the Communist International takes place in Saint Petersburg and Moscow. The notorious Twenty-one Conditions are adopted.
- July 20 – The United Kingdom cedes its brief control of the key Black Sea port of Batum to the Democratic Republic of Georgia.
- July 22 – Polish–Soviet War: Poland sues for peace with Bolshevist Russia (refused).
- July 24 – Battle of Maysalun: The French defeat the Syrian army whose leader Yusuf al-'Azma is killed. French troops occupy Damascus and depose Faisal I of Syria as king.
- July 26 – Mexican Revolution: Pancho Villa takes over Sabina and contacts de la Huerta to offer his conditional surrender. He signs his surrender on July 28.
- July 29 – The United States Bureau of Reclamation begins construction of the Link River Dam as part of the Klamath Reclamation Project.
- July 30–August 8 – 1st World Scout Jamboree held at Olympia, London.
- July 31
  - Irish-born Australian Catholic Bishop Daniel Mannix is detained onboard ship off Queenstown and prevented from landing in Ireland or from speaking in the main

Irish Catholic communities elsewhere in the United Kingdom.
- ○ France prohibits the sale or prescription of contraceptives.
- ○ Representatives of British revolutionary socialist groups meet at the Cannon Street Hotel in London and agree to form the Communist Party of Great Britain.

August

- August 3 – Irish War of Independence: Catholic riots in Belfast in protest at the continuing British Army presence.
- August 10 – Ottoman Sultan Mehmed VI's representatives sign the Treaty of Sèvres with the Allied Powers, confirming arrangements for partitioning of the Ottoman Empire.
- August 11 – Bolshevik Russia recognizes independent Latvia.
- August 13–25 – Polish–Soviet War: The Red Army is defeated in the Battle of Warsaw.
- August 13 – Irish War of Independence: The Restoration of Order in Ireland Act, passed by the Parliament of the United Kingdom, receives Royal Assent, providing for Irish Republican Army activists to be tried by court-martial rather than by jury in criminal courts.
- August 19–25 – Second Silesian Uprising: The Poles in Upper Silesia rise up against the Germans.
- August 20 – The first commercial radio station in the United States, 8MK (WWJ), begins operations in Detroit. It is owned by the 'Detroit News, *the first U.S. radio station owned by a newspaper.*

- August 26 – The Nineteenth Amendment to the United States Constitution is passed, guaranteeing women's suffrage.

September

- September 5 – Presidential elections begin in Mexico.
- September 8 – Gabriele D'Annunzio proclaims the Italian Regency of Carnaro in the city of Fiume.
- September 16 – The Wall Street bombing: A bomb in a horse wagon explodes in front of the J. P. Morgan building in New York City, killing 38 and injuring 400.
- September 17 – The National Football League is established as the American Professional Football Association.
- September 20 – The first soldier joins *El Tercio de Extranjeros*, the "Regiment of Foreigners", later the Spanish Legion, established on January 28, in Spain; today is celebrated as the unit's anniversary. Under the command of José Millán Astray and Francisco Franco, its first duties are against Rif rebels in the Spanish protectorate in Morocco.
- September 21 – Communist Party of Uruguay is founded.
- September 22 – The London Metropolitan Police forms the Flying Squad, a motorised mobile detective patrol unit.
- September 27 – Polish–Soviet War: Bolshevist Russia sues for peace with Poland.
- September 29
  - The first domestic radio sets come to stores in the United States; a Westinghouse radio costs $10.
  - Adolf Hitler makes his first public political speech, in Austria.

October

- October 3 – Prix de l'Arc de Triomphe horse race first run in Paris.
- October 9 – Polish–Lithuanian War: Polish troops take Vilnius.
- October 10 – Carinthian Plebiscite: A large part of Carinthia Province votes to become part of Austria rather than Yugoslavia.
- October 14 – A peace treaty between the Soviet and the Finnish governments is concluded at Tartu.
- October 16 – Polish–Soviet War: After the Polish army captures Tarnopol, Dubno, Minsk, and Dryssa, the ceasefire is enforced.
- October 18 – Thousands of unemployed demonstrate in London; 50 are injured.
- October 26 – Álvaro Obregón is announced the elected president of Mexico.
- October 27 –
  - The League of Nations moves its headquarters to Geneva, Switzerland.
  - Baron Louis De Geer the younger becomes the new Prime Minister of Sweden.

November

- November 2
  - United States presidential election, 1920: Republican U. S. Senator Warren G. Harding defeats Democratic Governor of Ohio James M. Cox and Socialist Eugene

V. Debs, in the first national U.S. election in which women have the right to vote.
  - In the United States, KDKA AM of Pittsburgh (owned by Westinghouse) starts broadcasting as a commercial radio station. The first broadcast is the results of the presidential election.
- November 11 – The Unknown Warrior is buried in Westminster Abbey.
- November 13 – The evacuation of the White Army's last units and civilian refugees from the Crimea on board 126 ships, the remnants of the Russian Imperial Navy, to Turkey, Tunisia and the Kingdom of Serbs, Croats and Slovenes, accompanied by wide-scale civilian massacres. The total number of evacuees amounted to approximately 150,000 people, of which ~20% were civilians.
- November 14 – The Edmonton Symphony Orchestra holds its first concert.
- November 15 – In Geneva, the first assembly of the League of Nations is held.
- November 16 – Queensland and Northern Territory Aviation Services (*Qantas*) is founded by Hudson Fysh and Paul McGinness.
- November 17 – The council of the League of Nations accepts the constitution for the Free City of Danzig.
- November 21 – Irish War of Independence: Bloody Sunday: The Irish Republican Army, on the instructions of Michael Collins, shoot dead the "Cairo gang", fourteen British undercover agents in Dublin, most in their homes. Later that day in retaliation the Auxiliary Division of the Royal Irish Constabulary open fire on a crowd at a Gaelic Athletic

Association Football match in Croke Park, killing thirteen spectators and one player and wounding 60. Three men are shot this night in Dublin Castle "while trying to escape".

- November 28 – Irish War of Independence: Kilmichael Ambush: The flying column of the 3rd Cork Brigade of the Irish Republican Army, led by Tom Barry, ambushes two lorries carrying men of the Auxiliary Division of the Royal Irish Constabulary at Kilmichael, County Cork, killing seventeen (with three of its men also dying), which leads to official reprisals.

December

- December 1 – The Mexican Revolution ends with a new regime coming to power, which couples with the end of the Old West.
- December 5 – A referendum in Greece is favorable to the reinstatement of the monarchy.
- December 10 – Irish War of Independence: Martial law is declared in Counties Cork, Kerry, Limerick and Tipperary.
- December 11 – The Burning of Cork in Ireland: British forces set fire to some 5 acres (20,000 m²) of the centre of Cork, including the City Hall, in reprisal attacks after a British auxiliary is killed in a guerilla ambush.

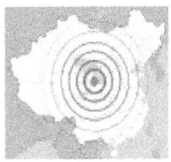

Haiyuan earthquake

- December 16
  - Finland joins the League of Nations.
  - An 8.6 Richter scale Haiyuan earthquake causes a landslide in Gansu Province, China, killing 180,000.
- December 15–22 – The Brussels Conference establishes a timetable for German war reparations intended to extend for over 42 years.
- December 22 – The 8th Congress of Soviets of the Russian SFSR adopts the GOELRO plan, the major plan of the economical development of the country.
- December 23
  - United Kingdom and France ratify the border between French-held Syria and British-held Palestine.
  - Government of Ireland Act 1920, passed by the Parliament of the United Kingdom, receives Royal Assent from George V providing for the partition of Ireland into Northern Ireland and Southern Ireland with separate parliaments, granting a measure of home rule.
- December 25 – The Rosicrucian Fellowship's spiritual healing temple *The Ecclesia* is dedicated at Mount Ecclesia, Oceanside, California.

Date unknown

- Hydrocodone, a narcotic analgesic closely related to codeine is first synthesized in Germany by Carl Mannich and Helene Löwenheim.

- Approximate date – The HIV pandemic almost certainly originates in Léopoldville, modern-day Kinshasa, the capital of the Belgian Congo.

Births

January

Javier Pérez de Cuéllar

Federico Fellini

DeForest Kelley

- January 1
  - José Antonio Bottiroli, Argentinean composer and poet (d. 1990)
  - Virgilio Savona, Italian singer and songwriter (d. 2009)
  - Heinz Zemanek, Austrian computer pioneer (d. 2014)
- January 2
  - Isaac Asimov, American author (d. 1992)
  - George Herbig, American astronomer (d. 2013)
  - Anne-Sofie Østvedt, Norwegian resistance leader (d. 2009)
- January 3
  - Renato Carosone, Italian musician and singer (d. 2001)
  - Abbas Ali, Indian freedom fighter and politician (d. 2014)
- January 5 – Arturo Benedetti Michelangeli, Italian pianist (d. 1995)
- January 6
  - John Maynard Smith, English biologist (d. 2004)
  - Early Wynn, American baseball player (d. 1999)
- January 7 – Vincent Gardenia, American actor (d. 1992)
- January 9
  - Clive Dunn, British actor (d. 2012)
  - Hakim Said, Pakistani scholar and philanthropist (d. 1998)
- January 12 – Bill Reid, Canadian artist (d. 1998)
- January 15 – John O'Connor, American Catholic cardinal (d. 2000)
- January 16
  - Al Morgan, American novelist and television producer (d. 2011)

- Elliott Reid, American actor (d. 2013)
- Walter Frederick Morrison, American entrepreneur and inventor (d. 2010)
- January 19
  - Buddy O'Grady, American basketball player and coach (d. 1992)
  - Javier Pérez de Cuéllar, Peruvian Secretary-General of the United Nations
- January 20
  - Federico Fellini, Italian film director (d. 1993)
  - DeForest Kelley, American actor (d. 1999)
- January 23 – Gottfried Böhm, German architect
- January 24 – Jerry Maren, American actor
- January 27
  - Hiroyoshi Nishizawa, Japanese fighter ace (d. 1944)
  - Helmut Zacharias, German violinist (d. 2002)
- January 30
  - Michael Anderson, English film director
  - Delbert Mann, American television and film director (d. 2007)

February

Farouk of Egypt

Tony Randall

- February 2 – Heikki Suolahti, Finnish composer (d. 1936)
- February 3 – Henry Heimlich, American physician and medical researcher
- February 4 – Giriraj Kishore, Indian activist and politician (d. 2014)
- February 7
  - Oscar Brand, Canadian singer
  - An Wang, Chinese-born computer pioneer (d. 1990)
- February 11
  - Farouk I, King of Egypt (d. 1965)
  - Billy Halop, American actor (d. 1976)
- February 12
  - William Roscoe Estep, American Baptist historian (d. 2000)
  - Yoshiko Yamaguchi, Chinese-Japanese actress and singer (d. 2014)
- February 13
  - Seneka Bibile, Sri Lankan pharmacologist (d. 1977)
  - Annæus Schjødt, Jr., Norwegian barrister (d. 2014)
- February 17 – Ivo Caprino, Norwegian film director (d. 2001)
- February 18

- o Bill Cullen, American game show host (d. 1990)
- o Eddie Slovik, U.S. Army private (executed) (d. 1945)
- February 22 – Burt L. Talcott, American politician
- February 25 – Sun Myung Moon, Korean evangelist, founder of the Unification Church (d. 2012)
- February 26
  - o Tony Randall, American actor (d. 2004)
  - o Lucjan Wolanowski, Polish journalist, writer, and traveler (d. 2006)
- February 28
  - o Jadwiga Piłsudska, Polish pilot (d. 2014)
  - o Zaim Topčić, Yugoslav and Bosnian writer (d. 1990)
- February 29
  - o Howard Nemerov, American poet (d. 1991)
  - o Michele Morgan, French actress

March

James Doohan

- March 3
  - o James Doohan, Canadian-born actor (d. 2005)
  - o Ronald Searle, British cartoonist (d. 2011)
- March 4
  - o Jean Lecanuet, French politician (d. 1993)

- o Alan MacNaughtan, Scottish actor (d. 2002)
- March 5
  - o Rachel Gurney, British actress (d. 2001)
  - o Del Latta, American politician
- March 6 – Lewis Gilbert, British film director, producer and screenwriter
- March 9 – Franjo Mihalić, Croatian-Serbian athlete (d. 2015)
- March 10
  - o Alfred Peet, Dutch American entrepreneur, founder of Peet's Coffee & Tea (d. 2007)
  - o Boris Vian, French writer, poet, singer, and musician (d. 1959)
- March 11 – Nicolaas Bloembergen, Dutch physicist, Nobel Prize laureate
- March 14 – Hank Ketcham, American cartoonist (d. 2001)
- March 15
  - o Lawrence Sanders, American novelist (d. 1998)
  - o E. Donnall Thomas, American physician, recipient of the Nobel Prize in Physiology or Medicine (d. 2012)
- March 17 – Sheikh Mujibur Rahman, Founder of Bangladesh, first President & Prime Minister of Bangladesh (d. 1975)
- March 16 – Leo McKern, Australian actor (d. 2002)
- March 19
  - o Kjell Aukrust, Norwegian poet and artist (d. 2002)
  - o Paul Hagen, Danish actor (d. 2003)
- March 20
  - o Pamela Harriman, English-born United States diplomat, socialite (d. 1997)

- o Vickie Panos, Greek-Canadian female professional baseball player (d. unknown)
  - o Rosemary Timperley, British author (d. 1988)
- March 22
  - o Werner Klemperer, German actor (d. 2000)
  - o Albert H. Pearson, American farmer and politician (d. 1963)
- March 23 – Tetsuharu Kawakami, Japanese baseball player and coach (d. 2013)
- March 24 – Corbin Harney, elder and spiritual leader of the Newe (Western Shoshone) people (d. 2007)
- March 25
  - o Patrick Troughton, British actor (d. 1987)
- March 27 – Robin Jacques, English illustrator (d. 1995)
- March 31
  - o Deborah Cavendish, Duchess of Devonshire (d. 2014)
  - o Marga Minco, Dutch journalist and writer

April

Richard von Weizsäcker

- April 1 – Toshiro Mifune, Japanese actor (d. 1997)
- April 2 – Jack Webb, American actor, director, and producer (d. 1982)

- April 4 – Éric Rohmer, French film director (d. 2010)
- April 5
  - Barend Biesheuvel, Dutch politician, Prime Minister of the Netherlands from 1971 until 1973 (d. 2001)
  - Arthur Hailey, American writer (d. 2004)
- April 6 – Edmond H. Fischer, Swiss American biochemist, recipient of the Nobel Prize in Physiology or Medicine
- April 7 – Ravi Shankar, Indian sitar player (d. 2012)
- April 8 – Carmen McRae, American jazz singer (d. 1994)
- April 11
  - Emilio Colombo, 40th Prime Minister of Italy (d. 2013)
  - Peter O'Donnell, British author and writer of comic strips (d. 2010)
- April 12 – Buck Young, American actor (d. 2000)
- April 13
  - Roberto Calvi, Italian banker (d. 1982)
  - Liam Cosgrave, fifth Taoiseach of Ireland
  - Jack Lambert, American actor (d. 2002)
- April 15
  - Thomas Szasz, Hungarian-born psychiatrist and writer (d. 2012)
  - Richard von Weizsäcker, German politician, President of Germany (1984–1994) (d. 2015)
- April 16 – Prince George Valdemar of Denmark (d. 1986)
- April 19 – Gene Leis, American jazz guitarist and educator (d. 1993)
- April 20 – John Paul Stevens, American Supreme Court justice
- April 21 – Edmund Adamkiewicz, German footballer (d. 1991)

- April 22 – Valeri Petrov, Bulgarian poet (d. 2014)
- April 27 – Guido Cantelli, Italian conductor (d. 1956)
- April 29 – Harold Shapero, American composer (d. 2013)

May

Pope John Paul II

- May 2
  - Jean-Marie Auberson, Swiss conductor (d. 2004)
  - Otto Buchsbaum, Austrian-born writer and ecological activist (d. 2000)
  - Preben Neergaard, Danish actor (d. 1990)
- May 6 – Ratu Sir Kamisese Mara, first Prime Minister of Fiji and President of Fiji (d. 2004)
- May 7 – Rendra Karno, Indonesian actor (d. 1985)
- May 8 – Touko Laaksonen, Finnish artist, pseudonym Tom of Finland (d. 1991)
- May 8 – Saul Bass, American graphic designer (d. 1996)
- May 9
  - Richard Adams, English author
  - Mitsuko Mori, Japanese actress (d. 2012)
- May 11 – Denver Pyle, American actor (d. 1997)
- May 13 – Gareth Morris, British flautist (d. 2007)

- May 18
  - Pope John Paul II (d. 2005)
  - Lucia Mannucci, Italian singer (Quartetto Cetra) (d. 2012)
- May 20 – Domenico Leccisi, Italian politician (d. 2008)
- May 22 – Helen Andelin, American author (d. 2009)
- May 23 – Helen O'Connell, American singer (d. 1993)
- May 25 – Arthur Wint, Jamaican runner (d. 1992)
- May 26
  - John Dall, American actor (d. 1971)
  - Peggy Lee, American singer (d. 2002)
- May 28 – Gene Levitt, American television writer, producer, and director (d. 1999)
- May 29 – John Harsanyi, Hungarian-born economist, Nobel Prize laureate (d. 2000)
- May 30
  - Franklin Schaffner, American film and television director (d. 1989)
  - Shōtarō Yasuoka, Japanese writer (d. 2013)

June

- June 1 – Amos Yarkoni, Israeli soldier (d. 1991)
- June 2
  - Marcel Reich-Ranicki, German literary critic and member of the literary group Gruppe 47 (d. 2013)
  - Tex Schramm, American football executive (d. 2003)
  - Johnny Speight, British television scriptwriter (d. 1998)
- June 11 – King Mahendra, king of Nepal (d. 1972)
- June 12

- o Dave Berg, American cartoonist (d. 2002)
- o Jim Siedow, American actor (d. 2003)
- June 16
  - o Eva Estrada-Kalaw, Filipino politician,
  - o José López Portillo, President of Mexico (d. 2004)
- June 17
  - o Jacob H. Gilbert, American politician (d. 1981)
  - o François Jacob, French biologist, recipient of the Nobel Prize in Physiology or Medicine (d. 2013)
  - o Setsuko Hara, Japanese actress (d. 2015)
- June 18 Utta Danella, German writer (d. 2015)
- June 25 – Ozan Marsh, American pianist (d. 1992)
- June 26 – Jean-Pierre Roy, Canadian pitcher in Major League Baseball (d. 2014)
- June 29 – Ray Harryhausen, American animator (d. 2013)

July

- July 1 – Lucidio Sentimenti, Italian footballer (d. 2014)
- July 4
  - o Anthony Barber, British Conservative politician (d. 2005)
  - o Leona Helmsley, American hotel operator, real estate investor (d. 2007)
- July 10 – Owen Chamberlain, American physicist, Nobel Prize laureate (d. 2006)
- July 11
  - o Yul Brynner, Russian-born American actor (d. 1985)
  - o Zecharia Sitchin, Soviet-born American author (d. 2010)

- July 12 – Bob Fillion, Canadian professional ice hockey player (d. 2015)
- July 13
  - Don Ralke, American music arranger (d. 2000)
  - Bill Towers, English footballer (d. 2000)
- July 15 – Theresa Kobuszewski, American professional baseball player and World War II veteran (d. 2005)
- July 17
  - Juan Antonio Samaranch, Spanish International Olympic Committee president (d. 2010)
  - June Vincent, American actress (d. 2008)
- July 18 – Dolph Sweet, American actor (d. 1985)
- July 21
  - Constant Nieuwenhuys, Dutch painter (d. 2005)
  - Isaac Stern, Ukrainian-born violinist (d. 2001)
- July 24 – Bella Abzug, American feminist politician (d. 1998)
- July 25 – Rosalind Franklin, British crystallographer (d. 1958)

August

Maureen O'Hara

Shelley Winters

Ray Bradbury

- August 1
  - Sammy Lee, Korean-American diver
  - Thomas McGuire, American World War II fighter ace (d. 1945)
- August 2 – Hugh Hickling, English lawyer, colonial civil servant, law academic and author (d. 2007)
- August 3 – P. D. James, English mystery novelist (d. 2014)
- August 4
  - John Figueroa, Jamaican poet (d. 1999)
  - Helen Thomas, American author and news service reporter, member of the White House press corps and columnist (d. 2013)
- August 8
  - Leo Chiosso, Italian poet (d. 2006)

- ○ Jimmy Witherspoon, American singer (d. 1997)
- August 9 – Milton G. Henschel, American member of the Governing Body of Jehovah's Witnesses and 5th President of the Watch Tower Bible and Tract Society (d. 2003)
- August 10
  - ○ Ann Harnett, American female baseball player (d. unknown)
  - ○ Red Holzman, American basketball coach (d. 1998)
- August 16 – Charles Bukowski, American writer (d. 1994)
- August 17 – Maureen O'Hara, Irish-American actress (d. 2015)
- August 18
  - ○ Bob Kennedy, American baseball player and manager (d. 2005)
  - ○ Shelley Winters, American actress (d. 2006)
- August 21 – Christopher Robin Milne, English author and bookseller (d. 1996)
- August 22 – Ray Bradbury, American science fiction writer (d. 2012)
- August 26
  - ○ Mauri Favén, Finnish painter (d. 2006)
  - ○ Prem Tinsulanonda, Thai prime minister
- August 29
  - ○ Charlie Parker, African-American saxophonist and composer (d. 1955)
  - ○ Herb Simpson, American baseball player (d. 2015)

September

Mickey Rooney

- September 3 – Les Medley, English footballer (d. 2001)
- September 4 – Catherine Bennett, Canadian female professional baseball player
- September 10 – Fabio Taglioni, Italian motorcycle engineer (d. 2001)
- September 10 – Lore Lorentz, German cabaret artist/standup comedian (d. 1994)
- September 12 – Darussalam, Indonesian actor (d. 1993)
- September 14
    - Mario Benedetti, Uruguayan writer (d. 2009)
    - Cascarita [*a.k.a. Orlando Guerra*], Cuban music singer (d. 1975)
    - Lawrence Klein, American economist, Nobel Prize laureate (d. 2013)
- September 18 – Jack Warden, American actor (d. 2006)
- September 22 – William H. Riker, American political scientist (d. 1993)
- September 23
    - Mickey Rooney, American actor, dancer and entertainer (d. 2014)
    - Alexander Arutiunian, Armenian composer (d. 2012)

- September 24 – Dick Bong, American fighter ace (d. 1945)
- September 29 – Peter D. Mitchell, English chemist, Nobel Prize laureate (d. 1992)

October

Walter Matthau

Frank Herbert

Montgomery Clift

- October 1
  - Charles Daudelin, Canadian sculptor (d. 2001)
  - Walter Matthau, American actor (d. 2000)
- October 4 – Pietro Consagra, Italian sculptor (d. 2005)
- October 8 – Frank Herbert, American author (d. 1986)
- October 9
  - Jens Bjørneboe, Norwegian author (d. 1976)
  - Yusef Lateef, American jazz musician and composer (d. 2013)
  - Jason Wingreen, American actor (d. 2015)
- October 13 – Laraine Day, American actress (d. 2007)
- October 15 – Mario Puzo, American author (d. 1999)
- October 17
  - Claire Barry, American singer (The Barry Sisters) (d. 2014)
  - Montgomery Clift, American actor (d. 1966)
  - Miguel Delibes, Spanish novelist (d. 2010)
- October 19 – Pandurang Shastri Athavale, founder of the Swadhyay Movement (d. 2003)
- October 20 – Siddhartha Shankar Ray, Indian politician, Chief Minister of West Bengal (d. 2010)
- October 22 – Timothy Leary, American psychologist and author, proponent of LSD (d. 1996)
- October 23 – Vern Stephens, American baseball player (d. 1968)
- October 27
  - K. R. Narayanan, President of India (d. 2005)
  - Nanette Fabray, American actress, dancer and singer

- October 29 – Baruj Benacerraf, Venezuelan-born immunologist, recipient of the Nobel Prize in Physiology or Medicine (d. 2011)
- October 31
  - Dick Francis, British jockey-turned-novelist (d. 2010)
  - Joseph Gelineau, French composer (d. 2008)
  - Fritz Walter, German footballer (d. 2002)

November

Gene Tierney

- November 5
  - John H. Land, American politician, mayor of Apopka, Florida (d. 2014)
  - Douglass North, American economist (d. 2015)
- November 8
  - Sitara Devi, Indian dancer (d. 2014)
  - Esther Rolle, American actress (d. 1998)
- November 11 – Walter Krupinski, German World War II fighter ace and postwar general (d. 2000)
- November 12 – Josip Boljkovac, Croatian politician (d. 2014)
- November 13
  - Jack Elam, American actor (d. 2003)

- Georg Olden, African-American graphic designer (d. 1975)
- November 17 – George Dunning, cartoon director and animator (d. 1979)
- November 19 – Gene Tierney, American actress (d. 1991)
- November 21
    - Ralph Meeker, American actor (d. 1988)
    - Stan Musial, American baseball player (d. 2013)
- November 22 – Anne Crawford, British actress (d. 1956)
- November 25 – Ricardo Montalbán, Mexican actor (d. 2009)
- November 27 – Buster Merryfield, British actor (d. 1999)
- November 28 – Patrick Campbell Rodger, Scottish Anglican bishop (d. 2002)
- November 29 – Yegor Ligachev, Soviet politician
- November 30 – Virginia Mayo, American actress (d. 2005)

December

Clark Terry

Rex Allen

- December 1 – Peter Baptist Tadamaro Ishigami, Japanese Roman Catholic prelate (d. 2014)
- December 6
  - Dave Brubeck, American jazz pianist and composer (d. 2012)
  - George Porter, English chemist, Nobel Prize laureate (d. 2002)
- December 9 – Carlo Azeglio Ciampi, President of the Italian Republic
- December 10 – Stanko Todorov, Bulgarian communist politician (d. 1996)
- December 13 – Sally Mansfield, American actress (d. 2001)
- December 14 – Clark Terry, American musician and composer (d. 2015)
- December 17 – Ewa Paradies, German Nazi war criminal (d. 1946)
- December 19 – Little Jimmy Dickens, American country music singer/songwriter (d. 2015)
- December 21 – J. Roderick MacArthur, American businessman and philanthropist (d. 1984)
- December 24 – Yevgeniya Rudneva, Soviet World War II heroine (d. 1944)
- December 29
  - Josefa Iloilo, 3rd President of Fiji (d. 2011)
  - Viveca Lindfors, Swedish-American actress (d. 1995)
- December 30 – Jack Lord, American actor (d. 1998)
- December 31 – Rex Allen, American actor, singer, songwriter (d. 1999)

Possible

- Isaac Asimov, Russian-born author (born between October 4, 1919, and January 2, 1920, inclusive; d. 1992)

Date unknown

- Kim Yong-ju, North Korean politician, younger brother of Kim Il-Sung
- Cezmi Kartay, Turkish cicil servant and politician (d. 2008)

Deaths

January

Amedeo Modigliani

- January 2 – Paul Adam, French writer (b. 1862)
- January 3 – Zygmunt Janiszewski, Polish mathematician (b. 1888)
- January 4 – Benito Pérez Galdós, Spanish novelist (b. 1843)
- January 6
  - Heinrich Lammasch, Austrian statesman, last minister-president of Austria (as part of the Austro-Hungarian Empire) in 1918 (b. 1853)
  - Walter Cunliffe, English banker (b. 1856)

- January 6 – Hieronymus Georg Zeuthen, Danish mathematician (b. 1839)
- January 7 – Edmund Barton, Prime Minister of Australia (b. 1849)
- January 14 – John Francis Dodge, American automobile manufacturer (b. 1864)
- January 18 – Giovanni Capurro, Italian poet (b. 1859)
- January 22 – Georg Lurich, Estonian Greco-Roman wrestler and strongman (b. 1876)
- January 24
  - William Percy French, Irish songwriter and entertainer (b. 1854)
  - Amedeo Modigliani, Italian painter and sculptor (tuberculosis) (b. 1884)
- January 25 – Jeanne Hébuterne, French artist, model, and common-law wife of Amedeo Modigliani (suicide) (b. 1898)

February

Robert Peary

- February 2 – Field E. Kindley, American World War I aviator (b. 1896)
- February 3 – Frank Brown, Governor of Maryland (b. 1846)

- February 6 – Augustus F. Goodridge, Canadian merchant and politician (b. 1839)
- February 7 – Alexander Kolchak, Russian naval commander (b. 1874)
- February 11 – Gaby Deslys, French dancer, actress & spy (b. 1881)
- February 15
  - Aleksander Aberg, Estonian professional wrestler and strongman (b. 1881)
  - Joseph Burton Sumner, founder of Sumner, Mississippi (b. 1837)
- February 20
  - Robert Peary, American Arctic explorer (b. 1856)
  - Jacinta Marto, beatified, witnessed apparitions of the Blessed Virgin Mary in 1917 at Fátima, Portugal (b. 1910)
- February 27 – William Sherman Jennings, Governor of Florida (b. 1863)

March

- March 1
  - John H. Bankhead, U.S. Senator from Alabama (b. 1842)
  - William A. Stone, Governor of Pennsylvania (b. 1846)
  - Joseph Trumpeldor, Russian Zionist (b. 1880)
- March 3 – Theodor Philipsen, Danish painter (b. 1840)
- March 4 – Roswell P. Bishop, U.S. Congressman from Michigan (b. 1843)
- March 7 – Jaan Poska, Estonian barrister and politician (b. 1866)

- March 11 – Julio Garavito Armero, Colombian astronomer (b. 1865)
- March 15 – Rudolf Berthold, German World War I fighter ace (b. 1891)
- March 21 – Evelina Haverfield British suffragette (b. 1867)
- March 26
    - William Chester Minor, American surgeon (b. 1834)
    - Mary Augusta Ward, Tasmanian novelist (b. 1851)
- March 31
    - Paul Bachmann, German mathematician (b. 1837)
    - Lothar von Trotha, German military commander (b. 1848)
    - Edwin Warfield, Governor of Maryland (b. 1848)

April

Srinivasa Ramanujan

- April 1 – Walter Simon, German philanthropist (b. 1857)
- April 8
    - John Brashear, American astronomer (b. 1840)
    - Charles Tomlinson Griffes, American composer (b. 1884)

- April 10 – Moritz Cantor, German historian of mathematics (b. 1829)
- April 21 – Maria L. Sanford, American educator (b. 1836)
- April 26 – Srinivasa Ramanujan, Indian mathematician (b. 1887)

May

- May 1 – Princess Margaret of Connaught, Crown Princess of Sweden (b. 1882)
- May 10 – John Wesley Hyatt, American inventor (b. 1837)
- May 11
  - James Colosimo, Italian-born American gangster (b. 1878)
  - William Dean Howells, American writer (b. 1837)
- May 15
  - Owen Morgan Edwards, Welsh writer and educator (b. 1858)
  - Maria Bochkareva, Russian White soldier (b. 1889)
- May 16
  - Joselito, Spanish bullfighter (b. 1895)
  - Levi P. Morton, former Vice President of the United States (b. 1824)
- May 21
  - Venustiano Carranza, President of Mexico (b. 1859)
  - Eleanor H. Porter, American novelist (b. 1868)
- May 23 – Svetozar Boroević, Austro-Hungarian field marshal (b. 1856)
- May 28 – Hardwicke Rawnsley, English clergyman, poet, writer of hymns and conservationist (b. 1851)

- May 30 – George Ernest Morrison, Australian adventurer (b. 1862)

June

Max Weber

- June 5
    - Rhoda Broughton, Welsh writer (b. 1840)
    - Julia A. Moore, American poet (b. 1847)
- June 6 – James Dunsmuir, Canadian politician (b. 1851)
- June 13 – Essad Pasha, Prime Minister of Albania (b. 1863)
- June 14
    - Gabrielle Réjane, French actress (b. 1856)
    - Max Weber, German political economist (b. 1864)
- June 18
    - Jewett W. Adams, Governor of Nevada (b. 1835)
    - John Macoun, Irish born naturalist (b. 1831)
- June 20
    - Marie-Adolphe Carnot, French chemist, mining engineer, and politician (b. 1839)
    - John Grigg, New Zealand astronomer (b. 1838)
- June 27 – Adolphe-Basile Routhier, Canadian judge, author and lyricist (b. 1839)

July

- July 1 – Delfim Moreira, former President of Brazil (b. 1868)
- July 2 – William Louis Marshall, American general and engineer (b. 1846)
- July 3 – William Crawford Gorgas, American Army surgeon (b. 1854)
- July 5 – Max Klinger, German painter and sculptor (b. 1857)
- July 10 – John Fisher, 1st Baron Fisher, British admiral (b. 1841)
- July 11 – Empress Eugénie of France (b. 1826)
- July 14 – Albert Keller, German painter (b. 1844)
- July 17
    - Sir Edmund Elton, 8th Baronet (b. 1846)
    - Charles E. Courtney, American rower and rowing coach (b. 1849)
- July 22 – William Kissam Vanderbilt, American heir (b. 1849)

August

- August 1
    - Frank Hanly, Governor of Indiana (b. 1863)
    - Bal Gangadhar Tilak, Indian nationalist (b. 1856)
- August 2 – Ormer Locklear, American stunt pilot and film actor (b. 1891)
- August 9 – Samuel Griffith, Australian politician and judge (b. 1845)
- August 10
    - James O'Neill, American actor (b. 1847)
    - Ádám Politzer, Austrian otologist (b. 1835)

- August 12 – Hermann Struve, Russian-born astronomer (b. 1854)
- August 16
    - Henry Daglish, Premier of Western Australia (b. 1866)
    - Joseph Norman Lockyer, English astronomer (b. 1836)
- August 17 – Ray Chapman, baseball player (b. 1891)
- August 22 – Anders Zorn, Swedish painter (b. 1860)
- August 26 – James Wilson, Scottish-born American politician (b. 1835)
- August 31 – Wilhelm Wundt, German physiologist and psychologist (b. 1832)

September

Peter Carl Fabergé

- September 7 – Simon-Napoléon Parent, Premier of Quebec (b. 1855)
- September 10 – Olive Thomas, American actress (b. 1894)
- September 18 – Robert Beaven, Canadian politician (b. 1836)
- September 24 – Peter Carl Fabergé, Russian jeweler (b. 1846)
- September 25 – Jacob Schiff, German-born banker and philanthropist (b. 1847)
- September 30 – William Wilfred Sullivan, Canadian journalist, politician, and jurist (b. 1843)

October

- October 2
  - Winthrop M. Crane, Governor of Massachusetts and Senator (b. 1853)
  - Max Bruch, German composer (b. 1838)
- October 5 – William Heinemann, English publisher (b. 1863)
- October 7 – Yves Delage, French zoologist (b. 1854)
- October 10 – Hudson Stuck, English mountaineer (b. 1865)
- October 17
  - Reginald Farrer, English botanist (b. 1880)
  - John Reed, American journalist (b. 1887)
- October 24 – Grand Duchess Maria Alexandrovna of Russia (b. 1853)
- October 25 – Alexander of Greece, Greek king (b. 1893)

November

- November 1 – Kevin Barry, Irish republican (hanged) (b. 1902)
- November 2
  - Louise Imogen Guiney, American poet and essayist (b. 1861)
  - James Daly, Irish mutineer (firing squad)
- November 3 – Warren Terhune, United States Navy Commander, and the 13th Governor of American Samoa (b. 1869)
- November 4 – Ludwig Struve, Russian astronomer (b. 1858)
- November 9 – Alberto Blest Gana, Chilean novelist and diplomat (b. 1830)

- November 13 – Luc-Olivier Merson, French painter and illustrator (b. 1846)
- November 21 – Michael Hogan, Irish activist shot during a Gaelic football match by the British army, who also killed 14 Irish supporters (b. 1896)
- November 22 – Manuel Pérez y Curis, Uruguayan poet (b. 1884)
- November 23 – George Callaghan, British admiral (b. 1852)
- November 25
  - Madeline McDowell Breckinridge, leader of the women's suffrage movement and one of Kentucky's leading progressive reformers (b. 1872)
  - Gaston Chevrolet, Swiss-born race car driver and manufacturer (b. 1892)
- November 27 – Alexius Meinong, Austrian philosopher (b. 1853)
- November 30 – Eugene W. Chafin, American politician (b. 1852)

December

- December 11 – Olive Schreiner, South African writer (b. 1855)
- December 12 – Edward Gawler Prior, Canadian mining engineer and politician (b. 1854)
- December 14 – George Gipp, American football player (b. 1895)

Date unknown

- Manuel de la Cámara y Libermoore, Spanish admiral (b. 1835)

Nobel Prizes

- Physics – Charles Édouard Guillaume
- Chemistry – Walther Nernst
- Medicine – Schack August Steenberg Krogh
- Literature – Knut Hamsun
- Peace – Léon Victor Auguste Bourgeois

In the News.

Prohibition comes into force in the U.S

An **earthquake** measuring 8.5 magnitude on the Richter scale hits the heavily populated of Gansu province of China.

Influenza (the flu) and pneumonia spread Worldwide killing many thousands.

On November 11th The Tomb of The Unknown Warrior is buried in Westminster Abbey, London, signifying the soldiers killed during World War I who were not identified. It is the first example of a Tomb of the Unknown Soldier.

Small pox becomes a major problem worldwide.

The Summer Olympics are held in Antwerp, Belgium.

Inventions - Sticky Plasters, Hair Dryer, The Tea Bag and the Parachute.

Pancho Villa surrenders to the Mexican government.

The Ford Model T was continuing to sell well in the US.

1920 Calendar.

1920

January

	Sun	Mon	Tue	Wed	Thu	Fri	Sat
1					1	2	3
2	4	5	6	7	8	9	10
3	11	12	13	14	15	16	17
4	18	19	20	21	22	23	24
5	25	26	27	28	29	30	31

February

	Sun	Mon	Tue	Wed	Thu	Fri	Sat
6	1	2	3	4	5	6	7
7	8	9	10	11	12	13	14
8	15	16	17	18	19	20	21
9	22	23	24	25	26	27	28
10	29						

March

	Sun	Mon	Tue	Wed	Thu	Fri	Sat
10		1	2	3	4	5	6
11	7	8	9	10	11	12	13
12	14	15	16	17	18	19	20
13	21	22	23	24	25	26	27
14	28	29	30	31			

April

	Sun	Mon	Tue	Wed	Thu	Fri	Sat
14				1	2	3	
15	4	5	6	7	8	9	10
16	11	12	13	14	15	16	17
17	18	19	20	21	22	23	24
18	25	26	27	28	29	30	

May

	Sun	Mon	Tue	Wed	Thu	Fri	Sat
18							1
19	2	3	4	5	6	7	8
20	9	10	11	12	13	14	15
21	16	17	18	19	20	21	22
22	23	24	25	26	27	28	29
23	30	31					

June

	Sun	Mon	Tue	Wed	Thu	Fri	Sat
23			1	2	3	4	5
24	6	7	8	9	10	11	12
25	13	14	15	16	17	18	19
26	20	21	22	23	24	25	26
27	27	28	29	30			

July

	Sun	Mon	Tue	Wed	Thu	Fri	Sat
27				1	2	3	
28	4	5	6	7	8	9	10
29	11	12	13	14	15	16	17
30	18	19	20	21	22	23	24
31	25	26	27	28	29	30	31

August

	Sun	Mon	Tue	Wed	Thu	Fri	Sat
32	1	2	3	4	5	6	7
33	8	9	10	11	12	13	14
34	15	16	17	18	19	20	21
35	22	23	24	25	26	27	28
36	29	30	31				

Setptember

	Sun	Mon	Tue	Wed	Thu	Fri	Sat
36				1	2	3	4
37	5	6	7	8	9	10	11
38	12	13	14	15	16	17	18
39	19	20	21	22	23	24	25
40	26	27	28	29	30		

October

	Sun	Mon	Tue	Wed	Thu	Fri	Sat
40						1	2
41	3	4	5	6	7	8	9
42	10	11	12	13	14	15	16
43	17	18	19	20	21	22	23
44	24	25	26	27	28	29	30
45	31						

November

	Sun	Mon	Tue	Wed	Thu	Fri	Sat
45		1	2	3	4	5	6
46	7	8	9	10	11	12	13
47	14	15	16	17	18	19	20
48	21	22	23	24	25	26	27
49	28	29	30				

December

	Sun	Mon	Tue	Wed	Thu	Fri	Sat
49				1	2	3	4
50	5	6	7	8	9	10	11
51	12	13	14	15	16	17	18
52	19	20	21	22	23	24	25
53	26	27	28	29	30	31	

www.ingramcontent.com/pod-product-compliance
Lightning Source LLC
Chambersburg PA
CBHW071130280526
45787CB00003B/1229